Original title:
Supernova Sagas

Copyright © 2025 Creative Arts Management OÜ
All rights reserved.

Author: Thomas Sinclair
ISBN HARDBACK: 978-1-80567-807-6
ISBN PAPERBACK: 978-1-80567-928-8

The Song of Expanding Infinity

In the cosmos, a hiccup, bright and bold,
Stars are bursting, or so I'm told.
Galaxies giggle, they dance and twirl,
While comets slip on a cosmic pearl.

Planets wobble like jelly in space,
Aliens chuckle as they pick up the pace.
Rockets trip over their own saturn rings,
And aliens sing of improbable things.

Black holes burp, to everyone's surprise,
Swallowing snacks and sending out sighs.
Starlight chuckles, it's a sight to see,
As the universe laughs at its own jubilee.

So here's to the chaos, the comic delight,
Where everything's funny in the starry night.
Join in the laughter, let's share a few drinks,
In the great cosmic playground where madness winks.

Pulsing Stars in the Void

In a galaxy's witty retreat,
Stars tickle the darkness, oh so sweet.
They pulse like a heart with a big inner joke,
Dancing and laughing, like they're smoke.

With a wink and a twirl, they scatter light,
Hoping to make the blackness feel bright.
'What's a planet to do? We just shine,' they say,
Throwing confetti in the cosmic ballet.

Luminous Farewells

The cosmic bus is ready to roll,
Stars climb aboard to play their role.
They wave goodbye with a twinkling cheer,
Shooting out sparkles, spreading good humor here.

Galactic travelers don their best glow,
Chasing the light, they steal the show.
Packing humor in their stellar bags,
Floating through space like some cosmic nags.

Fragments of the Great Eruption

Caught in an explosion of giggles and glee,
Stars scatter like confetti, oh can't you see?
Each fragment a joke, in the cosmos wide,
Bursting laughter as they take a wild ride.

Like fireworks gone rogue, they bounce all around,
In the void, such hilarity is found.
Each glittering shard has its own crazy tale,
In the fun-filled void, they set out to sail.

A Light-Year Away

A light-year away, there's a party tonight,
Stars trading puns in the frosty starlight.
They sip on stardust, giggling with flair,
What is the universe? A giant funfair.

So when you gaze up, remember their glow,
Each twinkle a joke, each spark a "whoa!"
The cosmos rejoices, with laughter it sways,
In the warp of the void, where humor plays.

Shattered Galaxies

In a whirl of cosmic dust, so bright,
Stars trampoline with pure delight.
Planets dance in a zany waltz,
While comets giggle, laughing at faults.

Asteroids tumble, their paths misled,
A moon slips on its cheese, oh, dread!
Galactic mishaps, what a sight,
Universe hosts a comedic night.

Bright Echoes of Eons

A star sneezes, sending waves afar,
Jestful echoes from that twinkling star.
Black holes burp with a vortexy sound,
While starlight giggles as it swirls around.

Time travelers trip on their own shoelaces,
Caught in timelines with funny faces.
Regulars in this cosmic stand-up show,
Eons laughing, making time glow.

Celestial Ballads

Singing moons in a rock band unite,
Strumming stardust under cosmic light.
Saturn spins a tale so wild,
While Venus winks, oh, what a child!

Comets join in with tail feathers bright,
Creating rhythms that tickle the night.
The Milky Way joins with a dazzling sway,
While our planet pipes up, 'I've got something to say!'

Cosmic Reverberations

Jupiter tells a joke, oh so grand,
And Mars can't help but clap and stand.
The sun winks at the stellar crowd,
While galaxies giggle, joyful and loud.

Astro-critters spin tales unending,
With every twist, the laughter's bending.
In the void of space, joy resonates,
With interstellar laughs that reverberate.

Cosmic Constellations of Chaos

In the sky, a cat took flight,
Chasing tails of stars at night.
The moon sneezed, the sun chuckled,
While comets around them juggled.

Planets joined in cosmic prance,
Dancing in a wild, wobbly dance.
Aliens shouted, 'Hold my drink!'
As they floated, making stars blink.

Brightness Beyond Time

A star gave a wink, then it slipped,
Right off its axis, it flopped and flipped.
Galaxies giggled, they couldn't stop,
As one star yelled, 'Look, I just dropped!'

Time folded up like a paper plane,
Planets laughed till they were in pain.
Black holes grinned, 'This is our game!'
As light beams played a cosmic fame.

Constellation Chronicles

Once a bear with pants so old,
Strayed from the path, or so I'm told.
He bumped a star, made it snicker,
And tripped on a comet, it made him quicker.

Orion dropped his bow for a joke,
While a UFO burst out in smoke.
They argued over who wore it best,
As twinkling stars just couldn't rest.

Billowing Nebulae

In the clouds of dust, a whale swam free,
Singing ballads to a neighborly tree.
The comets laughed, and stars did cheer,
As their echoes danced across the sphere.

A nebula said with a twirl and a spin,
"Let's play hide and seek, come on, jump in!"
Lightyears later, they still play rounds,
While planets spin, creating funny sounds.

Temporal Illusions of Shining Dust

Stars are winking in a playful jest,
Brightly twinkling, never taking rest.
They play hide and seek, a cosmic tease,
Whispering secrets on the solar breeze.

Galaxies swirl in a merry dance,
Dropping stardust, they take a chance.
In a game of cosmic tag they play,
Who'll catch the light from yesterday?

Planets giggle as they spin around,
On merry-go-rounds of gravity bound.
With twirls and flips in a sight so grand,
Light years apart, still holding hands.

Cosmic jesters in the night sky, so bright,
Flying past comets, oh what a sight!
Each explosion a punchline in disguise,
As we laugh beneath these painted skies.

Dance of the Celestial Fiends

In the cosmos, mischief unfolds,
Fiends in the ether, so brave and bold.
They twirl and tumble in stellar delight,
Having a ball under the moonlight.

With a wink, they tie starry shoelaces,
Creating new constellations in races.
"Oops! Watch your step!" one giggles aloud,
As they frolic amongst the sparkling crowd.

The asteroids spin like dizzy old fools,
Playing hopscotch with cosmic rules.
"Last one to Mars is a rotten egg!"
They cheer and frolic with every leg.

Yet when the sun peeks, giggles grow faint,
Their antics subdued, like a gentle saint.
Till dusk brings the fun back, oh what a sight,
The dance of the fiends under velvet night.

Ascending Flames of Cosmic Fury

Blazing trails through the endless night,
Fiery bursts of laugh-inducing light.
Stars erupt like fireworks at a fair,
"Look out!" they shout, "Don't you dare stare!"

Cosmic chili, they bubble and pop,
Such spicy spirits, they just can't stop.
Each flare is a joke, a radiant tease,
Sparks fly higher, aiming to please.

As bright as a beacon, the comets race,
Slipping and sliding in a flaming embrace.
"Catch me if you can!" they squeal with cheer,
Astral mischief spreads far and near.

And when they fade, the cosmos sighs,
A laugh lingers on in the midnight skies.
For every blaze leaves a tale to tell,
Of laughter ignited, where bright embers dwell.

The Luminary's Silent Farewell

A star's last giggle, a wink goodbye,
Floating gently down from the sky.
With swirling sparkles and whispered cheer,
It leaves behind a twinkling tear.

As stardust drifts on the cosmic breeze,
It tickles moons and shakes the trees.
"Don't be sad," it seems to say,
"Watch me dance in a different way!"

Comets bow with a giggling nod,
In celebration of the playful odd.
"Here's to the spark that once shone bright,
We'll keep it alive in our shared light."

Then quietly fades the last of its glow,
Yet echoes of laughter in space still flow.
Though silent it goes, its jokes remain,
In the heart of the cosmos, like a sweet refrain.

Luminous Legends

In a sky where the stars do dance,
A star sneezed once, oh what a chance!
Galaxies twinkled with glee,
As space dust flew with wild esprit.

A comet with a neon tail,
Took a wrong turn and hit the ale.
It spun and twirled in a cosmic bar,
Making jokes with a twinkling star.

Planets laughed in the roundelay,
As meteorites joined the fray.
They juggled moons, all in good fun,
Under the light of a laughter sun.

So if you gaze up tonight,
And hear the stars chuckle in flight,
Remember their tales of jolly bursts,
In the universe, humor always bursts.

Eternal Ashes of the Firmament

In the depths of the cosmic soup,
A black hole made a surprising loop.
It burped out stars in a blazing splash,
Creating chaos with a cosmic crash.

While stardust formed a silly crew,
They strummed on rings, just for a few.
With laughter echoing through the void,
Gravity knew it was overjoyed.

One ancient quasar wore a hat,
It sat on a neutron star, imagine that!
The whole galactic crowd did cheer,
At such a style that brought them near.

So dance among the ashes here,
For they hold laughter, not just fear.
The firmament sways in giggles bright,
Where ashes spark with sheer delight.

A Cosmic Call to Adventure

In a rocket made of tinfoil dreams,
An astronaut shouted, "What are these beams?"
Galactic sirens, with glittery choir,
Called him forth to adventures higher.

On his way, he met a wise old moon,
Who sang a tune that made him swoon.
"Cross the asteroid's broken paths,
Avoid the space sharks, dodge their wrath!"

The planets threw a cosmic rave,
With disco balls that danced and waved.
They mixed their orbits to a funky beat,
Even black holes found two left feet!

With every twist, the laughter grew,
A stellar journey, bright and new.
Ashes of stars told stories bold,
As he soared through space, worlds unfold.

The Simmering Silence of Space

In the silence, there brewed a stew,
With alien chefs in hats of blue.
They stirred the cosmos with a spoon,
While planets hummed a merry tune.

A rogue meteor joined for the feast,
"Let's spice it up!" it said with a beast.
Black holes bubbled, sizzling bright,
While comets danced in sheer delight.

But silence erupted with laughter loud,
As quarks did flips, oh they were proud!
In the kitchen of stars, all was bright,
As culinary chaos took its flight.

So if you float in the vast unknown,
Remember the laughter sewn and sown.
For even in silence, joy can find,
A simmering space where fun's entwined.

Stardust Tales

In the cosmos, a cat's in a hat,
Chasing comets and a curious rat.
Stars giggle in the glittery sky,
As they dance, oh my, oh my!

Planets spinning, a merry mischief,
Jupiter's joke, oh what a sniff!
With rings so bright, Saturn can't hide,
While Earth just rolls, bouncing in pride.

Nebulas painting with colors so loud,
Aliens chuckle in a sparkling crowd.
Each twinkle a laugh, each blink a cheer,
In this universe, joy is always near.

So grab your telescope, come take a peek,
In this galaxy, we'll laugh till we squeak!
Amidst starlit fun, this is our craft,
For tails of stardust, watch the light daft!

The Fireworks of Oblivion

Galaxies pop like confetti in air,
Planets explode like they just don't care.
A comet sneezes, a supernova winks,
As black holes giggle and shine their blinks.

Here comes a star, spinning high with flair,
Stumbling through corners, like it's a fair.
With each galactic rumble, the cosmos shouts,
"Watch out for the meteors, watch out for doubts!"

Saturn's rings jingle, they rattle and roll,
While Mars plays hopscotch, that's his goal.
Laughter erupts, as the universe glows,
In this wild chaos, anything goes!

So load up the rockets, let's dance in the void,
With firework sparks, we'll never feel bored.
In this grand show, there's fun to be done,
For in outer space, we all share the fun!

Cosmic Epilogues

In the stillness of night, a shout from afar,
A shooting star slips on its own quasar.
With giggles and gasps, it lights up the scene,
As it bumps into planets, all covered in green.

Asteroids trip, and tumble they go,
Each one is a jester, stealing the show.
While Pluto, forgotten, plays tag with the sun,
Declares, 'I'm still here, let's all have some fun!'

A pulsar ticks in a rhythmic delight,
Counting the jokes in the deep of the night.
In the theater of space, no ticket we need,
Just laughter and stardust – that's all for the feed!

With cosmic wit, stars sketch their own fables,
As galaxies spin tales around shimmering tables.
Join in the chaos, let the stories arise,
In this vast universe, let's laugh 'til we rise!

Twilight of the Celestial Bodies

In twilight's glow, the stars start to play,
With chessboards made of moons on a beautiful day.
Mercury laughs, making Saturn's rings spin,
While Venus is giggling, like she's just won a win.

Oort Cloud's sleigh bells jingle in tune,
While comets burst in a lively cartoon.
The Milky Way winks at the humor it finds,
Gently teasing the gravity that binds.

A solar flare tickles the edge of a star,
Sending rays of laughter, oh how bizarre!
Even black holes, with their dark little grins,
Join in the fun where this cosmic dance wins.

So let's toast to the twilight, let giggles ignite,
For every great journey begins with delight.
In this universe, strange tales are spun,
With each twinkling laugh, we all have some fun!

The Twinkling of Celestial Destiny

In a galaxy far and wide,
Stars giggle, they cannot hide.
They wink at comets zooming past,
While planets spin and spin so fast.

In dance-offs, they twirl and sway,
Shooting stars join in the play.
A cosmic disco, oh so bright,
As aliens groove through the night.

Gravity's a prankster at times,
Pulling moons in silly rhymes.
Black holes munch on space debris,
Belching out with cosmic glee.

With every twinkle, laughter streams,
Infinite joy, or so it seems.
Each spark a joke that's out of sight,
In the vastness, pure delight.

Nebula's Silent Cry

In cosmic clouds, colors collide,
Nebulas laugh, their joy can't hide.
Yet sometimes they puff out a sigh,
But who can hear in the deep, dark sky?

They swirl and twirl in cosmic art,
Making clowns of every part.
A patchwork quilt that steals the show,
In the theater of space's glow.

Their silent cry is of delight,
As they tickle stars with pure twilight.
Wacky whispers ignite the void,
In the backdrop, laughter deployed.

Through vibrant hues, they try to say,
"Join our dance, let's slip away!"
A cosmic giggle, soft and rare,
Transporting all through the great air.

Echoes of Galactic Dissonance

In the void, where echoes roam,
Galaxies play a game of foam.
Each bloop and blorp a sound so grand,
While asteroids join in the band.

Comets can't hold back their charm,
Whizzing by with a wink and arm.
They crash and dance like silly fools,
In this cosmic realm, there are no rules.

The Milky Way hums a tune,
A jumbled mix beneath the moon.
The planets chuckle, sharing jokes,
As light-years stretch from silly folks.

In chaos bright, they shine and play,
Every note a cosmic bouquet.
Echoes bounce in galaxy's grip,
Ticklish sounds on a starlit trip.

Celestial Visions

In the sky, a canvas bright,
Planets giggle in sheer delight.
They paint with stardust, soft and light,
Creating visions that take flight.

With kooky shapes and vibrant hues,
They frolic in their playful views.
A fleeting wink, a dashing dash,
Cosmic laughter, a heavenly splash.

Stars in clusters play a game,
Chasing shadows, never the same.
Each twinkle is a burst of jest,
In the heavens, they are blessed.

Let's take a ride on a solar breeze,
Dance along with interstellar ease.
In visions bright, the cosmos grins,
As laughter flows where chaos begins.

The Lost Songs of Stars

In the galaxy's grand choir, they sing,
Yet one lost star forgot the lyrics, poor thing.
It hums off-key, like a cat in a hat,
While comets all chuckle, just look at that!

With asteroids dancing, it twirls around,
Spinning in circles, they all gather 'round.
A planet chuckles, 'Hey, join the show!'
But the lost star's tune is like a whoopee blow.

Laughter erupts in the night sky's embrace,
Even black holes can't help but join in the race.
For every cosmos, we dance and we sway,
To the tunes of the stars in their goofy display.

So, here's to the stars with their comical ways,
They shine above us through soft, starry haze.
Though some may be lost in a cosmic jest,
Their laughter lights up this universe best.

Cascades of Cosmic Color

The universe bursts in hues, oh so bright,
Planets throw parties with colors in flight.
Mars paints in red, as it twirls with grace,
While Saturn's rings giggle in polka dot lace.

Blue stars wear shades, sipping cosmic tea,
And yellow giants wobble, looking quite free.
In the nebulas swirl, with confetti of light,
Galaxies grin, what a colorful sight!

A rainbow of laughter spreads far and wide,
With meteors racing on a joyful ride.
As comets throw sprinkles in the vacuum's grand dance,
Even the quietest black holes join in the prance.

So here's to the colors that spill from the spheres,
A whimsical palette beyond all our years.
The cosmos is chuckling—a whimsical show,
In a cascade of colors, starry giggles flow.

The Silent Symphony of Space

In the void, there's a symphony, soft yet grand,
Where silence takes center, with a whimsical band.
Planets tap softly on celestial drums,
While quarks whisper secrets that no one becomes.

The vacuum vibrates with a silent cheer,
A comet's faint whistle fills space without fear.
Stars sway to the rhythm, their dance so sublime,
Filling the universe with giggles through time.

Gravity's pull plays a waltz with finesse,
While asteroids shuffle in a cosmic dress.
But the tunes stay hush-hush, otherworldly and sly,
As meteors tickle the night, oh my, oh my!

So raise up a toast to this quiet ballet,
Where silence sings louder than words in the fray.
In the vastness of starlight, our laughter aligns,
With the silent symphony, mystery twines.

Histories Between the Stars

Stars write their tales in the dark of the night,
With each twinkle giggling, they share in delight.
These cosmic historians scribble and scrawl,
Telling the tales of meteors with a brawl.

From ancient star wars to comies gone mad,
Every pulsar's a storyteller, oh so glad.
With histories tangled in light-years of fun,
A comet just winked, oh, this tale's just begun!

The universe chuckles at tales that were spun,
Like black holes that burp when the eat up a sun.
From super giant fables to neutron tweaks,
The cosmos giggles, through histories it speaks.

So here's to the legends that waltz through our skies,
With laughter and wonder, we gaze and we sigh.
For between all the stars, the fun never ends,
In the great cosmic book, a new laughter sends.

Echoes from the Heart of the Cosmos

In the cosmos, stars collide,
Planets giggle, comets slide.
A black hole grins, swirling might,
While aliens dance in disco light.

Galaxies spin with a twist and shout,
Nebulas puff, no shadow of doubt.
Asteroids hop like they're in a race,
What a show in this vast space!

Solar flares bubble, popcorn-like,
Quasars in pajamas, quite a sight.
Lost in the void, a sock drifts by,
What's it doing? Even stars sigh.

Cosmic jokes travel light years wide,
Only for us, can they confide.
So raise your glass to the night sky,
And laugh with stars as they wink and fly.

Fractured Light: A Celestial Tale

Light beams fracture, what a split,
A star forgot to pay its rent.
Gravity chuckles, pulling tight,
As planets play hide and seek at night.

In this tale of cosmic fun,
Meteorites search for a pun.
Galactic giggles fill the air,
While stardust sneezes without a care.

Jupiter's storms, a crazy dance,
Venus is too shy to take a chance.
Every twinkle, a wink in flight,
Who knew space could crack so bright?

Rockets zoom past with a cheer,
Why is nobody docked here?
Light-speed laughter echoes through,
Join the fun, there's room for two!

The Luminescence of Cosmic Wanderers

Wanderers roam with glowing trails,
Dancing in space with flailing fails.
Meteor showers, wishes gone wrong,
Uranus giggles, just holds on strong.

Stars wear shades, they're feeling cool,
Planets play tag, a silly duel.
Comets zoom in, what a glide,
"Life of the party," the moons confide.

Far-off aliens make balloon art,
Trying to win the galaxy's heart.
But one lost a bet, now stuck in a loop,
"Take me home!" calls out the cosmic troupe.

From one end to another they drift,
Seeking joy, a universal gift.
The night explodes with laughs and light,
In this cosmic circus, everything's bright!

Phoenixes of the Astral Depths

From the depths, a phoenix flies,
With sunglasses on, it starts to rise.
Wings of flame, but a flame that cools,
Chasing stardust and breaking rules.

In the void where silence reigns,
It juggles meteors, oh, what pains!
Flaring out with a giddy twist,
Even black holes can't resist.

Twirling around the cosmic thread,
Shooting antics we all dread.
With a wink, they burn and tease,
In this dance, the universe is pleased.

So let us join this stellar fest,
And soar through space, we'll give our best.
With laughter echoing through the dark,
Phoenixes ignite with a cosmic spark!

The Clarity of Collapse

When stars decide to take a dive,
They giggle and shimmer, oh what a vibe!
Gravity's a prankster, pulling tight,
Making bright bulbs go boom with delight.

In cosmic kitchens, pots bubble and pop,
Galactic chefs yell, "Don't let it drop!"
An apron of stardust guarantees flair,
As they serve up a banquet of cosmic rare.

Oh cosmic critters, in the night sky they play,
With wigs made of gas, in a dazzling display.
When one finally pops, oh what a scene!
A flash of sheer joy, in cosmic cuisine!

So when you look up, remember the fun,
Stars laughing and dancing, in each little run,
For the clarity of collapse isn't dread,
But a comic ballet of the luminous thread.

Remnants of Luminous Journeys

In the sky, hang old socks from a star's last trip,
They're twinkling and winking, take a cosmic sip!
Leftovers from journeys, oh what a mess,
A nebula party, in dazzling dress.

They've traveled the cosmos, seen things galore,
In a black hole bar, they won't ask for more,
With cocktails of light and starlit chats,
Laughing about ancient celestial spats.

The universe giggles at what once was grand,
Now just space junk, adrift, unplanned.
But remnants still shine, with a wink and a grin,
In this funny cosmos, where absurdities spin.

So toast to the journey, with a cosmic cheer,
For the tales of lost stars, we hold dear,
In the fabric of night, their laughter will stay,
As whispers of journeys that drifted away.

The Odyssey of a Dying Star

Once a giant, shining bright and bold,
Now it's more like a story that's getting old,
With a skip in its twinkle, it's losing its spark,
But oh dear friend, it's still quite a lark.

Its last hurrah's a cosmic high five,
A farewell dance, as it starts to dive,
Gasps of the universe, a funny applause,
For the star's grand finale, without a pause.

Where does it go when the lights fade away?
It jokes with black holes, 'Let's play hide and sway!'
In the cosmic club where celestial dwell,
Stars share their stories, a funny farewell.

So here's to the star, with a wink and a grin,
Its Odyssey ends, but the laughter begins,
In the depths of the night, it isn't quite done,
Just a cosmic comedian, still having fun.

Infinity's Lamentation

Oh infinity, you tease us so sweet,
With endless horizons, a cosmic repeat,
But your jokes grow old, just like a bad pun,
In an eternal loop, there's no way to run.

The stars sit and ponder, 'What's next, oh dear?'
With lightyears of laughter, they chug down the beer,
A cosmic café where time's just a game,
They giggle about how it's always the same.

So we dance with the light, chase shadows of dark,
In infinity's theater, each twinkle's a spark,
Yet sometimes we sigh, at this endless charade,
For even the cosmos needs a nice parade.

So let's find a planet, pull out some chairs,
Share stories of life while forgetting our cares,
Though infinity's endless, enjoy what you can,
For the joke's on the stars, in this cosmic plan.

Brightest Shadows of Nightfall

In the dark, the stars do twinkle,
Like a cat that's chased a sprink-
Ler of light, oh what a sight,
A cosmic dance of giggles bright.

Galactic pranks, the planets play,
Chasing comets all the way,
Meteors fall with a silly cheer,
"Catch that spark, we're all sincere!"

Asteroids in hula hoop spins,
Twirling 'round like goofy twins,
Holding hands in tug of war,
The moon just cringes, calls for more!

Black holes chuckle, eating light,
"Munching photons—what a bite!"
In this night, so full of glee,
Space is fun, just wait and see.

A Symphony of Solar Ashes

Ashes dance in cosmic breeze,
Playing tunes with such great ease,
While stars hum a silly song,
In the universe where we belong.

Solar flares do call and shout,
Jumping up and all about,
Wobbling like a dancer's grace,
Making echoes in empty space.

With each puff, a comet's tail,
Crafting jokes in stellar scale,
Laughing moons with wide-eyed cheer,
"Catch us if you think we're near!"

Galaxies swirl in twinkling jest,
Playing hide and seek, a cosmic quest,
In this vast and funny scene,
Where the universe is bright and keen.

Explosive Birth of Celestial Legends

From the dark, a burst of glee,
New stars shout, "Look at me!"
With a bang and a fizzy glow,
They pop up fast, like popcorn, whoa!

Nebulae in rainbow strings,
Dance around like living things,
Shooting stars with cheeky grins,
Heavenly pranks, oh where it spins!

Legends born from fire and fun,
Each a tale, each a pun,
Cosmic jokes in every flare,
Sharing laughs across the air.

The cosmos teems, a lively show,
Where everything is "Whoa!" and "Yo!"
In this birth of light and play,
Even planets laugh away the day.

The Last Breath of Stellar Giants

Oh, the giants take their bow,
With a cosmic sigh and a wow,
They puff out stars, a final jest,
Leaving behind their golden vest.

Spinning tales of outer space,
In their deep and booming grace,
"I had my fun, oh what a ride,
Now it's time to safely glide."

With a wink, they dim the light,
A grand farewell on this night,
The echoes of their laughter float,
In the void, like a silly note.

As they fade, they leave behind,
A universe of joy, entwined,
In every breath, a story told,
Of giants bold and spirits gold.

Chasing Shadows Across the Firmament

In the cosmos, I lost my cat,
He chased a comet, imagine that!
Now I search the Milky Way,
For that feline who loves to play.

Stars blink and giggle, oh so bright,
As I whimper under starlit night.
With a telescope, I look in vain,
For my kitty must be quite the brain!

I bump into planets—what a sight!
They don't help; they just swirl with fright.
Shooting stars—are they a clue?
Or just fireworks for something new?

Finally, my cat comes back around,
When I'm tired and falling down.
"Did you have fun?" I confusedly ask,
He just purrs, avoiding the task.

Beyond Horizons: An Astral Odyssey

Floating on a balloon of dreams,
I peek at galaxies full of beams.
Venus winks with a golden grin,
While I ponder where to begin.

I packed a sandwich, a cosmic treat,
But aliens say that's quite a feat.
They brought me snacks from Mars, it's true,
But Space Cheese? Oh, what a goo!

Rocket fuel makes for vibrant dances,
In zero gravity, we take our chances.
A tumble here, a spin around,
Space's a park, where chaos is found!

Soon I trade my ship for a kite,
As stars giggle and take off in flight.
With every loop, I chase my fate,
In a dance with time—oh, what a date!

Celestial Orchestration

The stars form a band, playing with flair,
Jupiter jives, with gas in his hair.
Neptune's cool vibes make waves in the dark,
While Pluto insists he's still a great spark.

Moonlight whispers, "Let's sing a tune,"
As asteroids groove beneath the moon.
Saturn spins plates—what a unique show,
While comets swoosh by, stealing the flow.

The nebulae dance, all colors in play,
A cosmic festival—hip, hip, hooray!
Laughter erupts, echoes all around,
As constellations join, swirling sound.

At last, they wrap up with a final blast,
As I clap my hands, having a blast.
"Encore!" I shout, my spirit ablaze,
In this heavenly disco, I'll forever gaze.

A Symphony of Stars

Orion strums an ancient lute,
While Draco dances in a cute suit.
With every chord from Vega's glow,
The universe sways, putting on a show.

Pulsars thump like a cosmic drum,
While comets flash, "Come on, run!"
Starlight twinkles like a parade,
Each spark a playful serenade.

They gather round for the grand finale,
With Milky Way's glow, a celestial rally.
Nebulae join, painting the sky,
In colors so bright, you can't just pass by.

As the last notes fade into the night,
I giggle and grin at this starry sight.
In the orchestra of time, I take my seat,
Oh, how funny the cosmos can be, so sweet!

Phantom Light

A star played hide and seek at night,
But only shone when out of sight.
It winked and blinked with such delight,
While I just laughed at its ghostly flight.

It danced around my cosmic dreams,
With glitter and beams like liquid creams.
But when I reached, it split at seams,
Leaving me lost in stardust seems.

I tried to catch a glowing wisp,
But all I got was a hefty lisp.
The stars all chuckled at my grip,
As I floated off from the cosmic strip.

In the end, with cosmic pranks unfurled,
I became the jest of the universe world.
So if you see that twinkling swirl,
Just know I'm laughing in a starlit whirl.

Orbiting Memories

In a galaxy far from the fridge,
I found a place to dance on the ridge.
With meteors falling like a wild binge,
I slipped and tripped near the space bridge.

Past planets spinning with frosty flair,
I recalled the days of my old chair.
With snacks and shows, we'd never despair,
Just rockets and laughter twinkling in air.

But now my chips float across the stars,
As I munch on dreams from the candy bars.
My friends, the comets, race in their cars,
Leaving trails of giggles and glittery jars.

So remember next time you lose a thought,
It's orbiting somewhere, it can't be caught.
Just follow the laughter, however distraught,
And know that in space, you're never forgot.

The Heartbeat of the Universe

The cosmos beats like a drum of joy,
With rhythms and tunes, oh boy, oh boy!
But sometimes it hums a silly ploy,
That sends us spinning like a toy.

Planets groove to the stellar beat,
As asteroids tap with tapping feet.
The sun struts by with a funky greet,
While black holes swirl, oh what a treat!

A comet swoops in, it brings the fun,
With tails of glitter, its dance begun.
But watch your snacks as they come undone,
For space is hungry when it's on the run.

So boogie with stars, let your spirits rise,
In the heartbeat of space, there's no disguise.
It's a cosmic party, no need for ties,
Just laughter and love that never dies.

Relics of Starlit Legends

I found a relic wrapped in light,
A legend of laughter that took flight.
With tales of gags through the endless night,
It tickled my fancies like a kite.

Old comets spin with tales so bold,
Of starry pranks and bright futures told.
They hiccup and stumble, oh what a fold,
In the galaxy of stories, the warmth never cold.

Asteroids whisper in cosmic lines,
Reciting jokes of ancient signs.
While quasars giggle with wibbly whines,
Crafting wonders beyond the pines.

So treasure the relics, embrace the lore,
For inside the universe, there's always more.
With a wink from a star, we'll all explore,
A journey of laughter forever to score.

Explosions in the Cosmos

In the dark of space, stars take a nap,
But one of them sneezed, oh what a mishap!
Dust and glitter flew far and wide,
And all the comets giggled, filled with pride.

A cosmic party broke out that night,
With asteroids dancing, oh what a sight!
Super-sized snacks, like moons and stars,
The universe shook with laughter from Mars.

Planets adorned in sparkly gowns,
While black holes spun tales of lost crowns.
Each explosion a punchline, bright and loud,
In the vast night sky where quirks abound.

So if you see a star flash and sway,
Just know it might be having a play!
In the cosmos, where humor's the key,
We laugh with the heavens, wild and free.

Radiance of the Infinite

A starlet twinkled, showing off flair,
While others complained, 'That's just not fair!'
Light-years stretched in a competitive race,
Who's the brightest? It's a comical chase.

Wobbling worlds are part of the show,
One bumped a comet, causing a glow!
With giggles and sparkles flung left and right,
The galaxy chuckles at the sheer delight.

Nebulas puffed out their colorful chests,
Claiming supreme as the space funny jest.
But as meteors tumbled, sparks flew by,
An intergalactic chuckle rose high.

So remember, dear friends, in the night sky,
The cosmos can jest, it's not just a sigh.
For in every flicker, each luminous thread,
Lies laughter so rich, it's joyly widespread.

The Dance of Dying Suns

Once upon a time, the suns had a ball,
Spinning and twirling, they wouldn't fall.
They high-fived planets with fiery flare,
While giggling space dust floated in the air.

A few suns at the back, ready to fade,
Shook their hips, saying, "Don't be dismayed!"
"Just because we're old doesn't mean we're done,
We're still shining bright—let's keep this fun!"

The light show continued with flares and laughs,
"Dance with us, comets!" The starry staff.
A moon broke out with spins and twirls,
As the universe swirled with sparkles and pearls.

And when it was time to dim their light,
Suns winked and said, "We'll be alright!"
For in dying, they sparked new life for awhile,
Turning darkness into a comic smile.

Galaxy's Final Whispers

In a galaxy far, where gossip is art,
The stars shared secrets, like it was a part.
"Did you hear about the moon's latest fling?"
"Oh please, it was just a foolish old thing!"

A whirlpool of stars began to conspire,
Whispers of supernova dreams never tire.
"Bet you a quasar it'll be a blast,
We'll throw a rave, make shadows outlast!"

Comets sped by, throwing confetti with glee,
While black holes grinned, "Just wait, you'll see!"
And as they combined for one final cheer,
The galaxies echoed with laughter sincere.

So when you gaze up and find such delight,
Remember the whispers of cosmic night.
For even as stars seem to sigh and dim,
The humor of space will forever brim.

When Galaxies Dance in Silence

In the cosmos, stars do sway,
Comets join a silly ballet,
Planets twirl with glittery flair,
Spinning sparkles fill the air.

Asteroids toss a cosmic pie,
While black holes hum a lullaby,
Nebulas giggle, soft and bright,
In a galaxy filled with light.

A dancing dwarf just slipped and fell,
Landing hard—oh, what a swell!
Shooting stars were caught in glee,
Wishing on their own marquee.

When silence reigns, the dance goes on,
Just a universe made of fun,
With laughter echoing through the night,
Galaxies prancing, hearts alight.

Radiant Reveries of a Dying Star

A star once bright, now wears a frown,
It's shedding layers, not a crown,
Giggling as it puffs out gas,
Becoming quite the glowing mass.

In its final show, it sways so wide,
With colorful puffs, it's a cosmic ride,
Twinkling jokes take flight with might,
A radiant end, what a sight!

Planets cheer, say, 'What a fuss!'
While meteors laugh, 'This is a plus!'
In the background, moons do prance,
As each new twinkle starts to dance.

Of fleeting beauty and vibrant hues,
It bids adieu with rather strange views,
A humorous end to a stellar plight,
As all gaze in awe, under night's light.

The Tapestry of Exploding Dreams

Throughout the cosmos, dreams ignite,
Arcane tales take off in flight,
With every pop and every bang,
The universe starts to sing and clang.

A cosmic quilt of stars and beams,
Sewing laughter into dreams,
As shooting stars create a scene,
Dancing laughter, wild and keen.

Amongst the chaos, a grin appears,
As stardust tickles cosmic spheres,
A super silly tale unfolds,
Of dreams exploding, joy untold.

The universe giggles, twinkling bright,
Crafting laughter in the night,
In this tapestry, fun prevails,
As laughter echoes through the trails.

Stellar Whispers in the Void

In the void, whispers float around,
Of stars in mischief, laughter abound,
A comet sneezes, sending dust,
While moons giggle as they adjust.

Cosmic rays play hide and seek,
Hiding behind asteroids, how they peek!
Galaxies gossip, spread the cheer,
A dark matter prank, oh dear!

A wink from a quasar, bright and bold,
As solar flares share secrets untold,
"Hey, did you hear what the black hole claimed?
It's the best at sucking! How it's famed!"

In this dark dance, laughter thrives,
In the void where humor survives,
Stellar whispers spin tales of fun,
In the vastness, we all are one.

Celestial Echoes of Distant Stars

In the night, they twinkle bright,
A dance of light, oh what a sight!
Falling fast, like a clumsy cat,
They trip through space, imagine that!

With a wink and a flick, they play their games,
Sending whispers, calling names.
A cosmic joke in the void so wide,
Are they laughing at us? Let's take it in stride!

In a universe where time takes a nap,
Stars spill secrets through a giant gap.
Some blink slow, while others zoom,
Like squirrels in orbit, making a ruckus in gloom!

Their shimmery glow lights up our dreams,
But watch your step, or so it seems.
One might poke you right in the nose,
And then, oh no, off it goes!

The Light That Fades Yet Shines

Dimmed by time, a sparkle might,
But don't you fear, it's still quite bright!
Like a grandpa star with a wink,
Dancing slowly, doesn't even blink.

The light plays tricks, a stellar tease,
Fading away with so much ease.
But when it sparkles, oh what a sight,
Like a disco ball in the dead of night!

Imaginary friends, they come and go,
Leaving behind a cosmic show.
"Oh look," they chuckle, "we've made a mess!
But isn't it fun to be a hot, burning stress?"

With each flash, they hide and seek,
A cosmic game, not for the meek.
From wink to blink, a nightly spree,
Let's toast to stars, oh so carefree!

Cosmic Chronicles of Fiery Souls

In the oven of space, they bake and broil,
Fiery souls wrapped in cosmic foil!
With a giggle and a blaze so grand,
They're tossing stars like grains of sand.

Each soul a tale of wacky fate,
Floating 'round in a fiery state.
They roast marshmallows on solar flares,
"Oops! My snack fell! Who knows where?"

They gather round in a smoky haze,
Swapping stories from distant days.
"I once tried to outshine the sun,
But ended up with an overdone bun!"

A cosmic circus with luminous clowns,
While Jupiter chuckles and Saturn frowns.
In the galaxy's glow, we find our roles,
Dancing with laugh, those fiery souls!

Constellations Awakened and Torn

When stars collide, they make a mess,
Awakening clusters, I must confess.
Like startled cats in a midnight race,
They shuffle, tumble, and find their place.

Some stretch out lazy, some jump in fright,
Leaving trails of giggles in the night.
"Oh girly, is that a shooting star?"
"Nah, it just tripped over a cosmic bar!"

In a world of chaos where laughter flows,
Constellations clash, then strike poses.
With arms wide open, they take a bow,
"Thank you, Earthlings, we've graced you now!"

So when you gaze at the midnight scene,
Know the stars are crafting their funny routine.
A dance with fate, a space ballet,
Constellations awake, come join the play!

The Marvels of Dying Light

In the twilight, stars play hide and seek,
Even the sun says, 'This is quite unique!'
A cosmic clown with a twinkle and a grin,
Winks at the moon, 'Are you coming in?'

Galaxies swirl in a dance of delight,
With comets that crash, oh what a sight!
Planets giggle and wobble in their race,
While black holes joke, 'Don't forget your space!'

The universe chuckles, a vast, endless prank,
Lightyears pass by with a tinkle and clank.
The cosmos tickles the stardust we share,
As laughter erupts in the vacuum of air!

And as the last light begins to recede,
Stars leave their jokes like a cosmic seed.
In the silence that follows, we learn to embrace,
The humor of endings in interstellar space.

Celestial Paradoxes

In a spinning wheel, the planets all tease,
Saturn shouts, 'Look at my rings, I'm a breeze!'
Mars throws a party, 'Come join the fun!'
While Venus rolls eyes, 'I've already won!'

Time's just a joker, a trickster at best,
Who says, 'What's the hurry? You're all just a guest!'
Earth wonders, 'Is it Monday or noon?'
While the stars all just giggle and hum a soft tune.

Neptune is pouting, says, 'No one can see!'
As if a great secret is just for the sea.
Lightwaves will dance, both far and quite near,
In a cosmic ballet, it's laughter we hear!

And in the paradox, humor takes flight,
While space unfolds wonders, both silly and bright.
With every twist woven, a smile starts to form,
In the laughter of galaxies, we find our warm norm.

The Voyager's Lament

Oh Voyager, you're lost in the stars,
Zooming past Pluto and counting the scars.
'The more that I travel, the less that I know,'
You mutter to asteroids, 'Does it ever slow?'

Your message in bottles, a cosmic old jest,
'Hello, Earthlings. I must confess!'
They laugh at your woes, as you drift far away,
'Next stop, a black hole – what a wild lay!'

Photo of Earth, you wave as you roam,
'Who knew the Milky Way would feel like home?'
Yet time stretches long, and data drips slow,
Says the cosmic fill-in, 'Hey, can we go?'

But Voyager smiles, in silence it beams,
Crafting its path through the vast, endless dreams.
A rebel of space, not lost but just free,
With laughter of stardust, 'Just let me be!'

Flicker of Distant Dreams

A flash in the night, what could it be?
A star playing tricks in the cosmic spree.
It twinkled so bright, then gave a sly wink,
'We're all just a joke, don't you think?'

Nebulas giggle, come watch the parade,
As constellations get lost in charades.
Orion forgets where he parked his bow,
While Ursa the Bear steals the show with a growl!

In puddles of light, the cosmos unwinds,
Echoes of laughter flow through the finds.
Time ticks on silly, with stars to confide,
In the vastness of space, we all laugh and glide.

So here in the flickers, our dreams intertwine,
With humor in darkness, a spark that will shine.
In the end, as we drift, just remember this theme,
In the dance of the cosmos, we're all part of the dream!

The Burning of the Cosmos

In a galaxy not too far,
Stars gathered for a cosmic bazaar.
They sold jokes and comets, oh what a sight!
One star tripped, and it lit up the night!

Planets danced, and moons did a jig,
While asteroids hooted, looking quite big.
A black hole laughed, with a vibrant whoosh,
It swallowed a star, saying, 'What a goosh!'

The cosmos was warm, jokes flew in the air,
As rockets zoomed by, without a care.
Galactic giggles echoed wide,
And the universe chuckled, stars never hide!

So if you look up, and the stars seem to jest,
Know in their hearts, they're all having a fest!
With laughter and light, they shine bright and free,
In a universe that's silly as can be!

Astrological Odes

Oh look, the stars are writing a song,
About the moon who thought she was strong.
But her glow was really just a bright bulb,
Making wishes go wild, what a hubbub!

Mars wore a cape, looking quite dapper,
While Venus danced, causing quite the clapper.
They formed a band, the 'Galactic Boys',
Singing sweet tunes and making loud noises.

Jupiter turned up with rings of delight,
Claiming he's king of the cosmic night.
The stars all giggled, in twinkling chats,
"No one outshines us, you big old brat!"

In this celestial fest with humor galore,
The planets kept laughing 'til they could take no more.
With comets as dancers, a spacey parade,
In the galaxy's band, their fun never fade!

Enigmatic Event Horizons

Something strange happened near the old void,
A black hole giggled, feeling quite annoyed.
It tried to pull in a rogue little star,
But instead got a planet, oh what bizarre!

The planet cried out, 'What's this big mess?'
'Is it a ride or a cosmic stress test?'
The black hole just laughed, 'Oh, don't you fret,
We'll make a vortex, the best one yet!'

Across the universe, stars blinked in glee,
Watching this chaos, as wild as can be.
They tossed popcorn at comets flying by,
As the black hole twirled, it nearly said 'why?'

In the midst of the whirl, the laughter was real,
A cosmic quirk that made them all squeal.
So if you hear giggles in the night sky,
Just know that it's fun, oh my, oh my!

The Veil of Light

A curtain of starlight draped across the night,
Where giggling galaxies danced with delight.
They played hide and seek behind the moon's glow,
With laughter so bright, it put on quite a show!

One star yelled, 'Catch me, I'm quick as a flash!'
While another, much slower, made a big splash.
The Sun just sighed, 'Can't you hold still?'
But stars keep twirling, it's too much fun, chill!

A nebula jumped in, with colors so bold,
Spreading the joy, making starlight unfold.
With bursts of confetti, and comets that cheer,
The cosmos is laughing; it's crystal clear!

So next time you gaze at the veil up above,
Know it's just stars, sharing giggles and love.
A cosmic party where the light flares ignite,
Creating a tapestry, a funny delight!

The Bursting Heart of Space

In a galaxy not so far,
A star did burst, oh what a spar!
Cosmic popcorn, skies in fright,
Laughing atoms danced all night.

Gravity flipped, round and round,
Stars wore hats that twirled and frowned.
Aliens snickered in their ships,
Sharing cosmic popcorn trips.

A comet slipped on cosmic grease,
Too much speed? Oh, what a feast!
With each explosion, giggles grew,
Space was laughing, who knew who?

And when it ended, all was bright,
Stars threw parties, what a sight!
In the chaos, joy did bloom,
In heart of space, there's always room.

Starry Night's Farewell

Stars waved goodbye, they left in haste,
Whirling like dancers, oh what a taste!
A sunbeam tickled the Milky Way,
"Oh no!" it laughed, "Not another day!"

Planets tripped on their own tails,
Stepping on comets, making trails.
Laughter echoed through the dark,
As meteors played hide and spark.

The moon winked, feeling sly,
"Catch me if you can!" it cried.
With a pirouette, it spun away,
Stars clamored, "Let's join the fray!"

In the silence, giggles flowed,
Cosmos bursting with jokes bestowed.
So when you look up at skies so wide,
Remember the laughs that stars abide.

Chronicles of Cosmic Ruin

Once upon a time, a star grew fat,
A belly so big, it loved to chat.
Said "I'll burst, and what a boom!"
But all that echoed was a balloon!

Galactic gossip spread so fast,
Stars placing bets on how long it'd last.
'Round and 'round, they held the line,
Hoping it would tip their wine.

Black holes giggled, having a ball,
While comets slipped and started to fall.
"Let's break the laws of cosmic norm!"
They shouted and twisted like a storm.

Not a single planet took a pause,
Celebrating chaos without a cause.
In the end, all burst with glee,
In the cosmos, there's room for spree!

Cosmic Dreams in Freefall

In the realm where space does twist,
Dreams can tumble, not to be missed.
A star decided to roll and dive,
"Let's soar high, feel alive!"

Through asteroids, with a wink,
Flying fast, they'd barely blink.
But cosmic butterflies whispered sweet,
"Don't forget to watch your feet!"

A galactic breeze gave a silly shove,
Stars held hands, just like a glove.
And when they landed, oh what a glee,
Rolling on galaxies, wild and free!

So if you gaze at night's dark slide,
Remember dreams that laugh and glide.
For in the cosmos, joy will reign,
In dreams of space, there's no such pain.

Elysium Amidst the Celestial Chaos

In a cosmic café, the stars sip tea,
Galaxies giggle, oh what a spree!
Asteroids skate on paths made of light,
While comets play tag in the endless night.

Planets in tutus dance with delight,
While the moon checks its hair, oh what a sight!
Neutron stars laughing, 'What's gravity for?'
As chaos reigns on this celestial floor.

In this galactic circus, all is grand,
With black holes hiding, they've formed a band.
Each pulsar winks, a cosmic tease,
Spinning tales of fun like a cosmic breeze.

So join the crowd in this twilight glow,
Where stars tell jokes, and comets flow.
A universe laughing, a radiant charm,
In Elysium, oh, there's no harm!

Star-Fall Chronicles

Once a star tripped on its own bright tail,
Fell through the cosmos like a comical sail.
'Oops!' it exclaimed, 'What a big blunder!'
As planets looked on with wide-eyed wonder.

While shooting stars trade their best lines,
Confetti of stardust falls and shines.
Galactic giggles echo through space,
As meteors race in a joy-filled chase.

Asteroids joke, 'We're just space rocks!'
Cracking wise as they twirl in flocks.
The universe chuckles, 'A funny show!'
As gravity whispers, 'Where'd they go?'

In this tangled tale of cosmic cheer,
Shooting stars waltz with nary a fear.
The chronicles of humor, they brightly beam,
In this vast sky of whimsical dreams.

Twilight Radiance

Under the twilight, stars take a bow,
With a wink and a nod, they're here, oh wow!
A sunbeam giggles, 'I do love to tease,'
While planets play hopscotch with cosmic ease.

In the silence of night, a nebula hums,
While Milky Way whistles, oh how it strums!
Constellations sketching their playful art,
With Orion throwing a comical dart.

Planets spin tales, their voices a blend,
As starlight laughs, "On me you can depend!"
Twilight brings laughter, a show of delight,
In a radiant cosmos, everything feels right.

With the universe smiling, it's clear to see,
That in this vast space, there's fun to be.
So dance with the stars, enjoy the embrace,
In twilight's glow, there's joy in this place.

Light Conduits of the Past

From the whispers of time, bright beams emerge,
Past stars and moons in a lighthearted surge.
Galactic memories tickle the night,
As comets reminisce, taking flight.

'Remember when we danced?' a quasar jokes,
While all the old stars share laughter and pokes.
Wormholes giggle at their twisted paths,
Creating connections that spark cosmic laughs.

In the relics of light, stories intertwine,
Astrophysical giggles, oh, how they shine!
Each photon a prank, a tale to tell,
In this light-filled cosmos, all is well.

So let's toast to those days, with starlit cheer,
Where laughter rings out for all to hear.
In the conduits of light, joy is the cast,
In the funny forever, we're all unsurpassed.

The Time Capsule of Cosmic Events

In a capsule floating up high,
Aliens peek in, oh my!
They giggle at Earth's silly things,
Like cats and dogs with diamond rings.

They took a selfie with a star,
Wondering if it traveled far.
With tinfoil hats, they laugh with glee,
Earthlings are wild, oh can't you see?

Their ship runs on cosmic ice cream,
Every flavor's a wacky dream.
But chocolate swirls make engines stall,
As they drift by Jupiter's grand ball.

They sent a postcard back to us,
"Keep feeding your space cat, no fuss!"
Laughter echoes through the night,
In this cosmic, quirky flight.

A Journey Through the Radiant Abyss

Let's venture where the colors clash,
A universe where rainbows splash.
A place where socks have minds of their own,
And planets sing with a funny tone.

Asteroids dance a jolly jig,
While stars spin tales, both silly and big.
Their glow is bright, but watch your step,
On comets that offer a wobbly pep!

We met a worm in a disco ball,
Who boogied hard, and had a ball.
"Join me, friend," he'd cheer with zest,
"Let's shimmy our way through this cosmic fest!"

With giggles echoing in the void,
Even black holes can't be avoided.
They swirl with humor, never distress,
In this radiant, joyful mess.

Flickers of Life in Distant Realms

A flicker here, a twinkle there,
Life pops up, but beware!
Space fish wearing funky hats,
Play tag between the starry spats.

On Venus, they hold tea parties,
And discuss the latest space marties.
With biscuits that crunch like asteroids,
Their laughter evades all voids.

One critter claimed to invent light,
But really just glowed in the night.
They wrote a book, "How to Shine,"
With tips on wiggles and the best wine!

Floating past moons that never sleep,
Worms and rays make secrets to keep.
In realms afar, the fun won't stop,
With comets and dreams, it's a joyous hop!

Galactic Legacies written in Light

Cosmic tales are spun with cheer,
Each glow and shimmer we hold dear.
From silly stars to quirks that rise,
In the vastness where laughter flies.

Planets play tricks, oh what a sight,
With moons on roller skates at night.
A game of tag upon the rings,
While shooting stars trade funny things.

Galaxies whisper secrets sweet,
Not just of fates, but of cosmic feats.
They giggle at our earthly cares,
And light up skies with silly flares!

In the cosmic book of legacy,
Laughter echoes for all to see.
As starlit chuckles fill the space,
We celebrate the universe's grace!

Capturing Celestial Fire

In the night sky, stars wink and jest,
One twinkling burst puts us to the test.
Cosmic chaos, it spins and swirls,
A dance of gas, and watch it twirls.

A cat on a comet, in slippers it slides,
Through interstellar ice, where humor abides.
Giggles echo in the void so wide,
As planets spin out in a cosmic ride.

Watch the astronomers drop their charts,
As radiant flares burst forth in parts.
They scramble in laughter, with telescopes askew,
While planets laugh back with a chuckle or two!

So catch a glimpse of this jovial mess,
A fiery show, nothing less than blessed.
When stars conspire in a glittery haze,
We toast to the night, in a funny blaze!

Tapestry of the Universe's End

In the fabric of night, a stitch appears,
With cosmic threads spun from our fears.
But wait! What's that? A thread gone loose,
Comet's tail tickles, oh what a ruse!

A gigantic needle, through galaxies weaves,
As stars pull pranks, oh don't be naive!
One flares up, shouting "Catch me if you can!"
While we laugh, thinking, "Oh what a plan!"

They weave their tales of galactic delight,
With puns and quips, what a sight!
The universe giggles, bursting in style,
A comedic quilt, one star at a while.

But as the end nears, we'll toast with a grin,
For even in darkness, the fun will begin.
We'll laugh with the cosmos, no calamity here,
For joy is eternal, it's crystal clear!

When Suns Burst Forth

A bright star yawns, stretched wide and long,
With a sleepy smile, it hums a song.
"Oops! I did it again!" it cheekily beams,
As solar flares burst, igniting our dreams!

The sun cracks jokes in its fiery tone,
While planets groan, "Oh here we go, alone!"
Storms of giggles in cosmic embrace,
While asteroids tumble, oh what a race!

See Neptune slip on a swirling blue beam,
While Mercury fumbles with an awkward gleam.
The cosmos erupts, it's pure comedy gold,
As planetary antics are forever retold.

So when suns burst forth with glee undisguised,
Mark the sky's laughter, don't be surprised.
For in the vastness, with each bright display,
The universe chuckles, come join in the play!

Nebulous Narratives

In a cloud of gas where stories collide,
The universe giggles, with nowhere to hide.
A tale of mischief, of stars out of place,
Hilarious antics, a whimsical chase!

"Who sat on my tail?" did a neutron complain,
"Two black holes tangoed! Oh what a bane!"
The dwarf stars chuckled with twinkling delight,
While comets threw snacks in a mid-space fight!

Lost in a nebula's playful embrace,
Celestial characters join in the race.
The fabric of space filled with laughter's refrain,
As gravity pulls at our smile, we gain!

So gather your stardust, let's spin a new yarn,
Where cosmic mischief rules like a charm.
For in this vast sketch of stellar cheer,
Nebulous narratives bring joy near!

www.ingramcontent.com/pod-product-compliance
Lightning Source LLC
Chambersburg PA
CBHW071851160426
43209CB00003B/509